WRITTEN AND ILLUSTRATED BY
Shauna Mooney Kawasaki

SALT LAKE CITY, UTAH

Visit us at deseretbook.com

ISBN 1-59038-232-3

Printed in the United States of America
Publishers Printing, Salt Lake City, UT

72076-7178

10 9 8 7 6 5 4 3 2 1

Introduction

The First Presidency has taught that "happiness in family life is most likely to be achieved when founded upon the teachings of the Lord Jesus Christ" ("The Family: A Proclamation to the World," *Ensign*, November 1995, 102). During the year 2004, Primary children throughout the world will learn about families and the lasting joy that comes from knowing families can be forever. Through sharing time presentations, classroom lessons, and Primary singing time, children will learn why "the family is central to the Creator's plan for the eternal destiny of His children" (ibid.).

This book is designed to help Primary presidencies, teachers, and parents follow the 2004 Sharing Time Outline and monthly themes set forth by the Primary general board. Each chapter correlates with one of the twelve areas of focus for the year. Chapters contain ideas for simple activities that are appropriate for very young children, as well as ideas for more elaborate activities that can take place in the classroom or at home. Artwork can be used to make word searches, dot to dots, flannel board stories, concentration games, word puzzles, and other popular children's activities. Scripture references and Primary songs are incorporated into many of the activities. All songs referenced in this book can be found in the *Children's Songbook* (Salt Lake City: The Church of Jesus Christ of Latter-day Saints, 1989).

Much of the artwork in the book can be used for multiple purposes. Photocopying, coloring, cutting, laminating, and employing your own creativity are encouraged as you use this book to enhance your lessons, sharing time presentations, and family home evenings. You may want to review the entire book before using any of the activities. This way, you will be familiar with the types of activities outlined here and thus be able to modify any activity to fit your particular needs and lesson topic. Each chapter includes a shaded box with an object lesson that will help to make your teaching experience—and your children's learning experience—more rewarding.

The CD-ROM that accompanies this book contains all of the artwork seen here. Artwork is listed on the CD-ROM by page number and is ready to export to your favorite word processing or page-layout program. It is permissible to print, photocopy, trace, enlarge, or otherwise reproduce the materials in this book for personal use at home or in the classroom (not for distribution).

To install the art on your computer's hard drive, follow the instructions printed on the face of the CD-ROM. Feel free to use your creativity in adapting any of the ideas and concepts in this book. It is hoped that you will find them a valuable resource in your important work of helping children learn about the Savior and his role in their lives and the happiness of their families.

1 I Am a Child of God

We are children of our Heavenly Father. He loves us and wants us to return to live with him. He blessed us with many things when we chose to come to earth: family, scriptures, prophets, and our Savior.

Use the activities on pages 3 through 6 to help children understand that they are sons and daughters of a loving Heavenly Father.

Page 3. Make a copy of one of the figures on page 3 for each child. Have the children color and cut out their figures. Help with the leg holes if necessary. For small children, you may want to cut out the images ahead of time.

After the children have colored their pictures, show them how to put two fingers through the leg holes and turn the figures into puppets. Talk about different prayers, who says them, and where they are said. Remind the children that prayer is a reverent way to talk to our Father in Heaven. Bear your testimony of prayer. Tell the children their prayers will always be answered in the way Heavenly Father thinks best.

Page 4. Prepare a copy of page 4 for each child. Have the pianist play soft music while the children unscramble the words in the handout. All of the words are names for Jesus Christ. Provide help when necessary. Discuss why Jesus Christ was chosen to come to earth as our Savior, what he did while he was here, and how he sacrificed for us. Remind the children to take their papers home to share with their families.

Page 5. Prepare a copy of page 5 for each child. Talk about how we are created in the image of our Heavenly Father and how our bodies are a wonderful gift, given to every spirit that comes to earth. Use the scriptures to help the children understand that our bodies are temples and should be cared for and treated properly (see 1 Corinthians 3:16–17). Pass around a mirror and have each child look in the mirror and then draw a self-portrait on the handout. Remember to fill in the spaces for names and the date. This would be a good keepsake in a book of remembrance.

Page 6. Use this page in a variety of ways:

- As a coloring page after a discussion about our blessings here on earth
- As pictures for a roller box presentation
- As cards for a concentration game
- As cards for a "blessings bag." Color and cut out the images on the straight lines. Fold the pictures in fourths and put them in a paper bag. One at a time, draw them out and have different children talk about what Heavenly Father has given us to show his love for us.
- As a flip chart for a talk or presentation

OBJECT LESSON

Topic: We are Heavenly Father's children, created in his image
Object: Mirrors
Scripture: James 1:22–24

Tell the children that Heavenly Father loves us. We are his children created in his image. We can show our thanks and love for him by remembering where we come from, respecting our bodies, and remembering that our bodies are very precious.

Let everyone have the opportunity to look in the mirror. Talk about how the reflection in the mirror is what people see when they look at us. We take good care of that image by bathing, combing our hair, and brushing our teeth. But we need to take care of our "inside reflections" too. Heavenly Father sees our spirits, not just our outer appearance. Through prayer, scripture study, good works, and choosing the right, our inside image or reflection will shine through, and those around us will see who we really are—children of God.

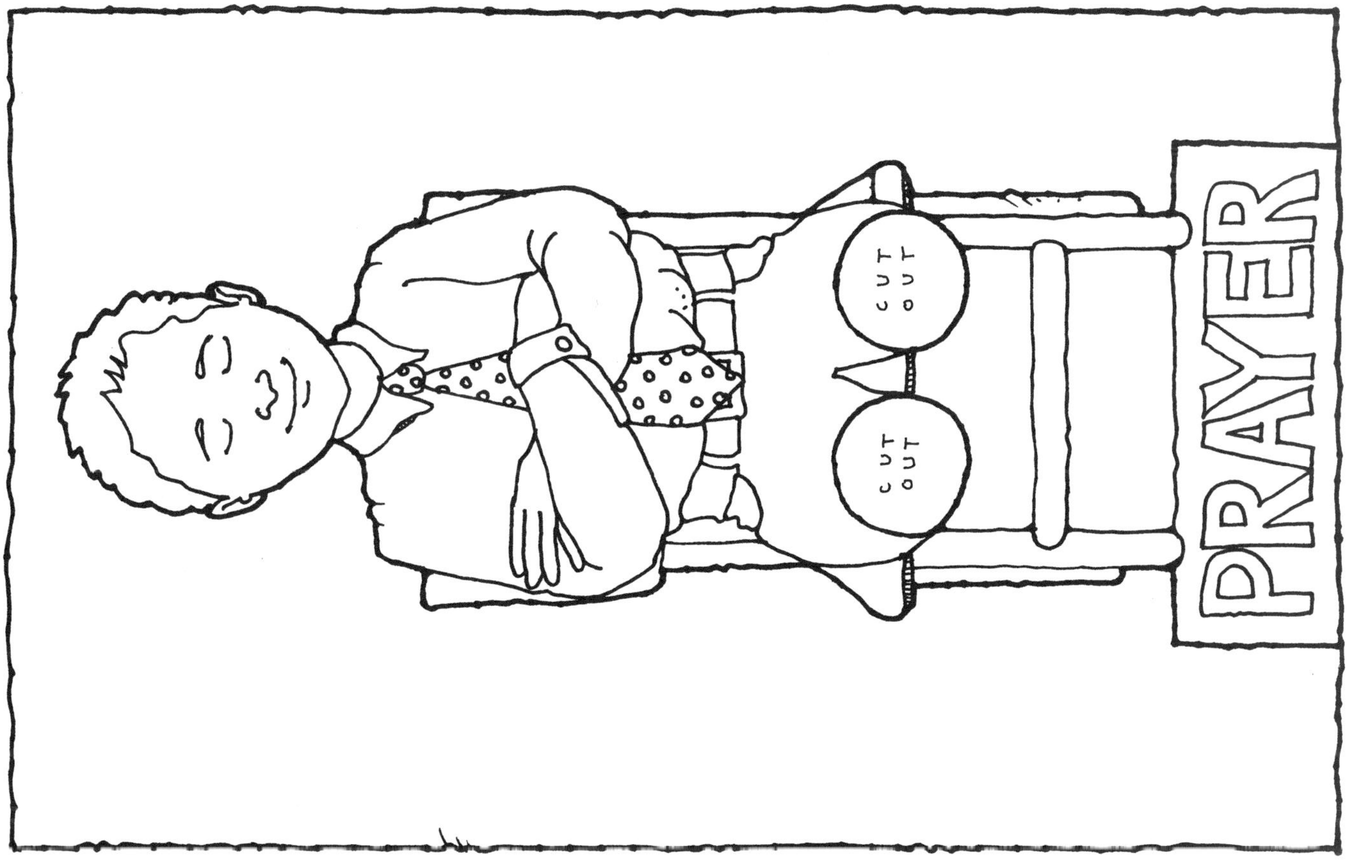

CUT OUT

CUT OUT

PRAYER

CUT OUT

CUT OUT

PRAYER

NAMES OF CHRIST

UNSCRAMBLE THE WORDS, USING THE SCRIPTURE REFERENCES FOR HELP IF NEEDED. ALL OF THE WORDS ARE NAMES FOR JESUS CHRIST.

AND THE SON OF GOD WAS THE SSEMHAI _ _ _ _ _ _ _ WHO SHOULD COME 1 NEPHI 10:17

HIS VOICE WAS AS THE SOUND OF GREAT WATERS, EVEN THE VOICE OF VAEHJOH _ _ _ _ _ _ _ D&C 110:3

I AM THE DOGO HHEPESRD _ _ _ _ _ _ _ _ _ _ _ _ _ AND THE ESTON OF RSIEAL _ _ _ _ _ _ _ _ _ _ _ D&C 50:44

THE VOICE BEARING RECORD THAT HE IS THE NLYO TOTENBEG _ _ _ _ _ _ _ _ _ _ _ _ D&C 76:23

I AM THE URRTOIRESCNE _ _ _ _ _ _ _ _ _ _ _ _ AND THE LIFE JOHN 11:25

THE NKGI _ _ _ _ OF ALL THE TEARH _ _ _ _ _ AND ALSO THE KING OF EEVANH _ _ _ _ _ _ ALMA 5:50

I AM YOUR CADVEOTA _ _ _ _ _ _ _ _ WITH THE FATHER D&C 110:4

BEHOLD THE MABL _ _ _ _ OF OGD _ _ _ WHICH TAKETH AWAY THE SIN JOHN 1:29

I AM PLHAA _ _ _ _ _ AND GEAMO _ _ _ _ _ THE BEGINNING AND THE ENDING REVELATION 1:8

FOR HE WAS THE WORD, EVEN THE GNESSMERE _ _ _ _ _ _ _ _ _ OF SALVATION D&C 93:8

WHICH GLORY IS THAT OF THE CHURCH OF THE BRIRSTFON _ _ _ _ _ _ _ _ _ D&C 88:5

I AM THY SAVIOR AND THY REDEEMER, THE GHTYIM _ _ _ _ _ _ ONE OF BOJAC _ _ _ _ _ 1 NEPHI 21:26

MY BODY IS A TEMPLE

DRAW A PICTURE OF YOURSELF

MY HEAVENLY FATHER LOVES ME

2 The Family Is Central to Heavenly Father's Plan

No two families are alike. Behind every front door is a different set of circumstances: happy times, sad times, love, contention, growth, and change.

Our Father in Heaven wants us each to have love and happiness in our homes. This can be a very hard thing to do in this difficult, ever-changing, and confusing world.

Love, respect, and sharing are some things we can foster to bring peace into our homes. In "The Family: A Proclamation to the World" we are taught that a man and a woman should marry, have children, and then obey their sacred duty to raise those children in love and righteousness. It is no small thing to bring a child into the world, to love her, and to teach her correct principles so that she may return to her Heavenly Father. Each child deserves that love and respect. When we remember that we are children of our Heavenly Father, it is easier to show our love and respect for everyone.

Use the activities on pages 8 through 11 to help children understand that families are essential to Heavenly Father's plan and that we should treat our family members with love and respect.

Pages 8–10. Prepare a copy of page 8 for every child. Cut out the house and the door on the solid lines. Fold back the door on the dotted line. Put glue around the outside edges of the back of the house (not the door) and place atop another piece of paper. Before class, contact a parent or guardian of each child in your class and find out how many family members live in the child's house. Be sensitive to different situations. Prepare the appropriate number of copies of the figures on pages 9 and 10 for each student. Have the children color, cut out, and slip the family member figures inside each house. Discuss how everyone in the home has needs. If everyone helps and respects each other, there will be more love in the home. Give each child a house to take home.

Page 11. Make copies of the puzzle for each child. Do this activity during sharing time or class time, or send it home for the children to share at family home evening.

OBJECT LESSON

Topic: Our actions influence others
Objects: Warm water in a pitcher, a clear container or bowl, food coloring, ice cubes
Scripture: Alma 5:57

At the beginning of the lesson, put several ice cubes in a clear container, stating that the ice cubes represent each member of a family. Slightly melt the ice cubes by pouring warm water over them. Place one drop of food coloring into the container and stir it up. Continue to squeeze more drops in the container, stirring after each drop. Show the children that the ice cubes are starting to take on the colors of the food-coloring drops.

Talk about how every member of the family can make choices. If we make bad choices, it affects everyone and may soil the family name or make other members of the family unhappy. Talk about why we want to help our family have a "clean" name and how it will make us happier, our grandparents and ancestors happy, and our future children happy.

OUR HOME

LOVE AT HOME

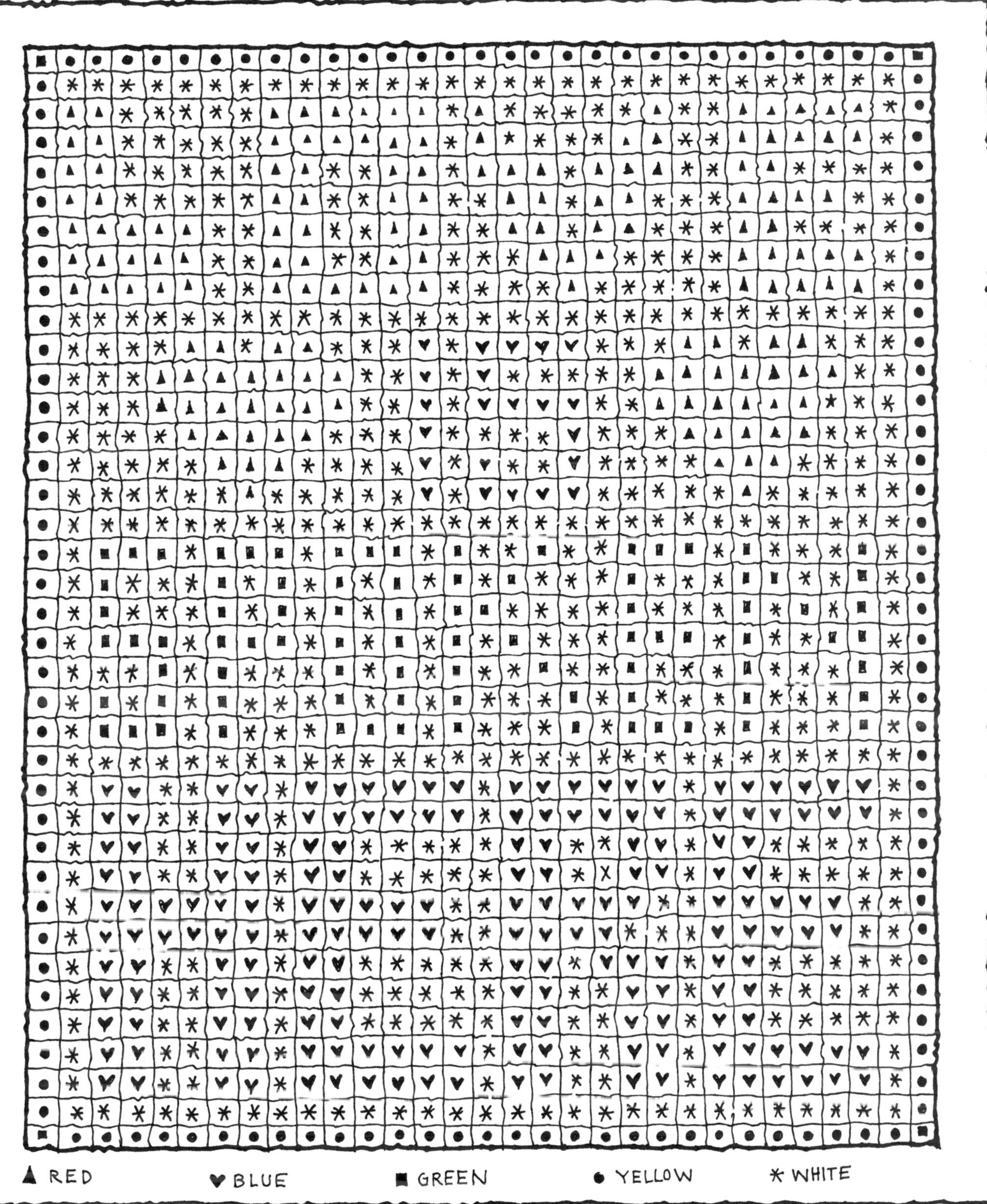

USING THE APPROPRIATE COLOR OF CRAYON, MARKER, OR COLORED PENCIL, FILL IN THE SQUARES THAT ARE MARKED WITH ONE OF THE ABOVE SYMBOLS.

3 Jesus Christ Makes It Possible for Me to Live with Heavenly Father Again

"For God so loved the world, that he gave his only begotten Son, that whosoever believeth in him should not perish, but have everlasting life" (John 3:16). Before any of us were born, we chose to come to earth and follow Heavenly Father's plan. Because we would make mistakes on earth, Heavenly Father needed someone to be our savior so we could repent and return to live with our Heavenly Father.

Heavenly Father sent Jesus Christ, our spirit brother, to be the Savior.

Use the activities on pages 13 through 16 to help children understand that Jesus' atonement makes it possible for us to return to our Father in Heaven.

Page 13. Prepare a copy of page 13 for each child. Color, cut out, and punch holes where indicated. Give each child a hanger, some string or yarn, and a set of circles. Have each child cut the string into 6 lengths, then tie one end of each string through the hole in each circle. Tie the other end of each string to a hanger to make a mobile. Talk to the children about how each of us is a spirit child of our Heavenly Father. Explain the phases of the plan of salvation as follows, showing the appropriate piece of the mobile as you discuss it:

1. *Pre-earth Life.* Before the earth was created, we lived with Heavenly Father. In this pre-earth life, Heavenly Father taught us about his plan and how we could become like him.

2. *Birth.* Eventually, each of us left the pre-earth life and the presence of our Heavenly Father. We were born on earth with a body of flesh and bones.

3. *Earth Life.* On earth, we have the chance to learn about the gospel and to make righteous choices.

4. *Death.* As our bodies become old, or sick, or are damaged by accidents or injuries, they stop working, and we die. At death our bodies and spirits are separated.

5. *Spirit World.* After we die, our spirits will go to the spirit world to receive further teachings.

6. *Life with Heavenly Father.* After our time in the spirit world, we will be resurrected and our spirits and physical bodies will be united. Those who are worthy will be able to live with Heavenly Father and Jesus.

Page 14. Enlarge, copy, and color page 14. Cut out the pictures along the solid lines. Make a flip chart by punching two holes at the top of each square. Secure the pages together with string or metal rings. On the board, write the scripture references that go with each picture for the children to look up as you use the pictures to tell the story of Jesus' life.

Page 15. Prepare a copy of page 15 for each child. Have the pianist play soft music while the children complete this activity. Encourage the children to take the message home and share it with their families.

Page 16. Prepare a copy of page 16 for each child. Have the pianist play soft music while the children complete this activity. Teachers and leaders can hum or sing the words very softly and encourage the children to also sing or hum as they are coloring.

OBJECT LESSON

Topic: We must follow a plan to achieve success
Object: Ingredients for a no-bake cookie recipe
Scripture: 2 Nephi 31:20

Display the ingredients for an easy no-bake cookie recipe. Talk about the functions of each ingredient as the children watch you mix up two batches: one with all of the ingredients, and one that leaves out something essential. Have two children taste the two different batches of cookies. Talk about why it is important to add all of the ingredients and what happens if one ingredient is left out. Compare this to the consequences of us not following Heavenly Father's plan. If a step is left out, will his plan work for us and our families?

PRE-EARTH LIFE
BIRTH
EARTH LIFE
DEATH
SPIRIT WORLD
LIFE WITH HEAVENLY FATHER

LIFE OF CHRIST

USE A CRAYON, MARKER, OR PENCIL TO FILL IN EVERY SPACE WITH A DOT IN IT. THE COMPLETED MESSAGE TELLS US WHAT WE CAN DO TO RETURN TO LIVE WITH HEAVENLY FATHER AND JESUS AGAIN.

GOOD OR BAD CHOICES?

COLOR THE PICTURES OF THE THINGS THAT WILL HELP YOU RETURN TO YOUR HEAVENLY FATHER. PUT AN "X" OVER THE CHOICES THAT WILL NOT MAKE YOU HAPPY.

4 Families Can Be Happy When They Follow Jesus Christ

Homes and families are the Lord's way of providing a social unit in which brothers, sisters, moms, and dads can teach, learn, and apply gospel principles. The Proclamation on the Family teaches us that "Happiness in family life is most likely to be achieved when founded upon the teachings of the Lord Jesus Christ" (*Ensign*, November 1995, 102).

Use the activities on pages 18 through 21 to teach children about how following Jesus' example can bring our families happiness and peace.

Page 18. Enlarge and color two copies of the beehive on page 18. Cut out the pieces of one beehive to make a puzzle. Pass the pieces out to the children and invite them up to the front of the room to put the puzzle together. Use the other copy as the background for the puzzle. You can use tape, pins, or magnets to secure the puzzle to the board. As the puzzle is put together, lead a discussion about President Gordon B. Hinckley's Nine Bs. (Six of the Bs come from a talk given on November 12, 2000 and published in the *Ensign*, January 2002, 2; the other three come from President Hinckley's book *Way To Be! Nine Ways to Be Happy and Make Something of Your Life* [New York: Simon and Schuster], 2002). Make a copy for each child to take home and share.

Page 19. Prepare a copy of page 19 for each of the older children. Review "My Gospel Standards" with the children before passing out the worksheet. Work as a group to put the right words in the blanks on the handout. Encourage the children to commit to and memorize "My Gospel Standards."

Younger children who cannot read can take turns guessing the words left out on the worksheet as you read each standard out loud. (Example: "I will use the names of ___ ___ and ___ ___ reverently.")

Page 20. Enlarge page 20 to poster size and place it on the board. Ask the children to look up Doctrine and Covenants 4:6 in their scriptures, or print it on the blackboard. Starting with the word *remember*, finish filling in the words from the scripture as they fit in the puzzle. Gently encourage and suggest answers. If you've written the scripture on the board, erase or cross out each word after it has been used. When the puzzle is complete, read it from the scriptures and memorize it together. Provide a copy for each child to take home and share with her family. (This activity works best with older children.)

Page 21. Enlarge and color the warning signs on page 21. Make each one a different color. Place the signs around the room. Choose one child to go out of the room. Have another child choose a sign. When the first child comes back in, the children should guide that child to the chosen sign by singing "Choose the Right Way" (*Children's Songbook*, 160). Sing softly when the child is far from the sign. Progressively get louder as the child gets nearer and then finds the correct sign. Talk about what the sign says and its warning. Continue until all of the signs are found.

OBJECT LESSON

Topic: Follow the light of Christ
Objects: Flashlight, blindfolds, and rope
Scripture: Alma 37:44

Stretch out a rope. Have each child hold it with her right hand. Darken the room and blindfold the students or have them shut their eyes until you tell them to open them. Have a teacher lead everyone around the room and a number of obstacles you have previously placed in the way. At the end of the "path," discuss the situation. Why was this hard to do? Was it dangerous? Did anyone get lost or have to peek? Repeat without obstacles and go in a straight line. Ask the children why it was easier this time. Repeat a third time with eyes open and the lights on. Ask how it was easier and safer this time. Tell the children that following the light of Jesus and listening to the Holy Ghost can bring them safely and peacefully to Heavenly Father just as the light helped them on their "path" in the Primary room.

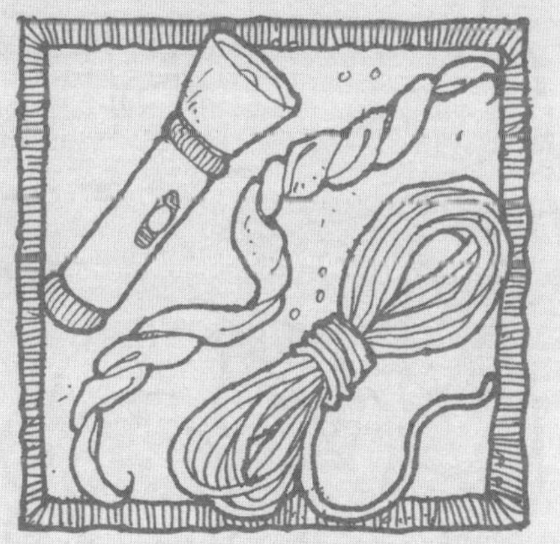

BE HAPPY
BE GRATEFUL
BE SMART
BE INVOLVED
BE CLEAN
BE TRUE
BE POSITIVE
BE HUMBLE
BE STILL
BE PRAYERFUL

GOSPEL STANDARDS

WRITE THE CORRECT WORDS IN THE BLANKS, USING THE NUMBERED CODE BELOW.

I will ㉞________ ⑧________ ________'s ㉟________ for me.

I will remember my ⑩________ ㉑________ and listen to the ⑥________ ________.

I will ㉔________ the ⑬________. I know I can ㉜________ when I make a ㉖________.

I will be ㉘________ with ⑧________ ________, ⑨________, and ①________.

I will use the ②________ of ⑧________ ________ and ⑯________ ________ ㉕________. I will not swear or use crude words.

I will do those ㉝________ on the ⑫________ that will help me feel ⑭________ to ⑧________ ________ and ⑯________ ________.

I will ⑱________ my ④________ and do my part to strengthen my family.

I will keep my ㉚________ and ③________ sacred and ⑰________, and I will not partake of ㉝________ that are harmful to me.

I will ㉗________ modestly to show ㉓________ for ⑧________ ________ and ①________.

I will only ㉙________ and ⑦________ things that are ⑪________ to ⑧________ ________.

I will only ⑤________ to ㉛________ that is ⑪________ to ⑧________ ________.

I will ⑳________ good ㉒________ and treat ⑨________ kindly.

I will live now to be ⑮________ to go to the ⑲________ and do my part to have an eternal family.

1. MYSELF	7. WATCH	12. SABBATH	18. HONOR	24. CHOOSE	30. MIND
2. NAMES	8. HEAVENLY FATHER	13. RIGHT	19. TEMPLE	25. REVERENTLY	31. MUSIC
3. BODY	9. OTHERS	14. CLOSE	20. SEEK	26. MISTAKE	32. REPENT
4. PARENTS	10. BAPTISMAL	15. WORTHY	21. COVENANT	27. DRESS	33. THINGS
5. LISTEN	11. PLEASING	16. JESUS CHRIST	22. FRIENDS	28. HONEST	34. FOLLOW
6. HOLY GHOST		17. PURE	23. RESPECT	29. READ	35. PLAN

A GOOD RULE

USE YOUR DOCTRINE AND COVENANTS TO LOOK UP D&C 4:6.
PLACE THE WORDS FROM THAT VERSE WHERE THEY FIT IN THE PUZZLE.

WATCH FOR THE SIGNS

STOP
THAT WHICH IS EVIL COMES FROM THE DEVIL.
SEE OMNI 1:25

SLOW
YE SHALL NOT GO WITH HASTE, FOR THE LORD WILL GO BEFORE YOU.
SEE 3 NEPHI 20:42

CAUTION
YE WILL NOT SUFFER YOUR CHILDREN TO FIGHT ONE WITH ANOTHER.
SEE MOSIAH 4:14

YIELD
THE RIGHTEOUS YIELD TO NO SUCH TEMPTATIONS.
SEE ALMA 11:23

MERGE
NATURAL MAN MUST BECOME AS A CHILD, WILLING TO SUBMIT TO ALL THINGS.
SEE MOSIAH 3:19

DO NOT ENTER
NOTWITHSTANDING GOD'S GOODNESS AND MERCY, MEN SET AT NAUGHT HIS COUNSEL.
SEE HELAMAN 12:6

CAUTION
MEN ARE INSTRUCTED SUFFICIENTLY THAT THEY KNOW GOOD FROM EVIL.
SEE 2 NEPHI 2:5

X CROSSING
THERE IS OPPOSITION IN ALL THINGS.
SEE 2 NEPHI 2:11

5 Family Members Have Important Responsibilities

Family members should remember that we are all children of our Heavenly Father and that we knew each other in our pre-earth lives. We each have talents and special attributes that can be shared with each other as we contribute individually to our families.

Use the activities on pages 23 through 26 to teach the children about the important responsibilities of each family member.

Page 23. Enlarge and color page 23. Cut out on the heavy lines. On the back of the puzzle, number the pieces 1 to 9. Mix up the pieces and place them on the floor or table. Bring nine props from home for the children to wear as they pretend to be different members of a family. (For example: a doll for sister, a hat for brother, a tie for dad, a missionary tag for big brother, and so on.) Call nine children up to wear props. When they are dressed, have one at a time choose a puzzle piece and put it up on the board. Then the child in costume will tell what that family member does to help the family. Accept all answers. Continue until the puzzle is together. As a group, read the words around the border. Make a copy for each child to color and take home and share with his family.

Page 24. Prepare a copy of page 24 for each child. Cut each handout apart on the solid lines. Hand out a set of puzzle pieces and a blank sheet of paper to each child. Have the children "build" a home by gluing the pieces on the blank paper. You may want to enlarge the page for your own use as you teach the concept that a happy home is built on responsibilities. Start with the foundation of safety. Ask the children who has the responsibility to provide safety for the family. The next step is support. Ask the children what family members help to support the family. Accept all answers and remember to be sensitive to differences in each child's family. Teach the children that everyone in the family is responsible for providing love, comfort, and respect. When all of these blocks are put together, we have a happy home. Encourage the children to share this with their families.

Page 25. Prepare a copy of page 25 for each child. Have two children come to the front of the room and act out each scene. Discuss how it would make someone feel to be treated rudely and without respect in the situations role-played. Have the children cut out the conversation balloons on the handout and glue them in the proper places. Young children will need help cutting. Color the picture. Encourage the children to use good manners and nice words wherever they are—school, the playground, church, and especially at home.

Page 26. Enlarge the signs on page 26. Color them and cut them apart on the solid lines. Mount each sign on a separate stick. Use the signs to help the children learn the songs for the 2004 Primary Sharing Time Program. While the children sing a song, hold up different signs to instruct the children on how to—or who should—sing the song. You could also give a copy of the page and a set of sticks to each child to take home and use in family home evening.

OBJECT LESSON

Topic: Strong families
Object: Plastic Easter egg, small discs with key words written on them
Scripture: D&C 136:11

Write the word *family* on the plastic egg. Write some of the following words on small paper discs: be happy, peacemaker, clean up kitchen, clean up car, make bed, read scriptures, pray, help in yard, go to store, go to work, pay the bills, go to school, empty garbage, wash dishes, set the table, love one another, sing, cook meals, help with laundry, apologize, repent, honor, obey, protect.

Spread the discs out on a flat surface so none overlap. Have a volunteer put one hand behind his back and try to pick up all of the pieces with the other hand. Set a one-minute time limit for him. Replace the pieces and have another volunteer open the "Family Egg" and, using both hands, pick up all of the pieces and put them inside the egg.

Talk about the important responsibilities we all have and how we all need one another. As a family, we should do our best to help one another in accomplishing each individual task. Children should help mom so she can help them. Fathers should help children so that they can help mom. Heavenly Father wants us to support, honor, and love all of the people in our families.

FATHERS PRESIDE & PROTECT
CHILDREN HONOR & OBEY
EXTENDED FAMILY SUPPORTS US
MOTHERS NURTURE US

HOME

RESPECT

COMFORT

LOVE

SUPPORT

SAFETY

MANNERS SHOW RESPECT

Please?

Thank you.

I'm sorry.

May I help?

He did it.

Help please.

COLOR THE PICTURES. CUT OUT THE CONVERSATION BALLOONS AND GLUE THEM IN THE PROPER PLACES.

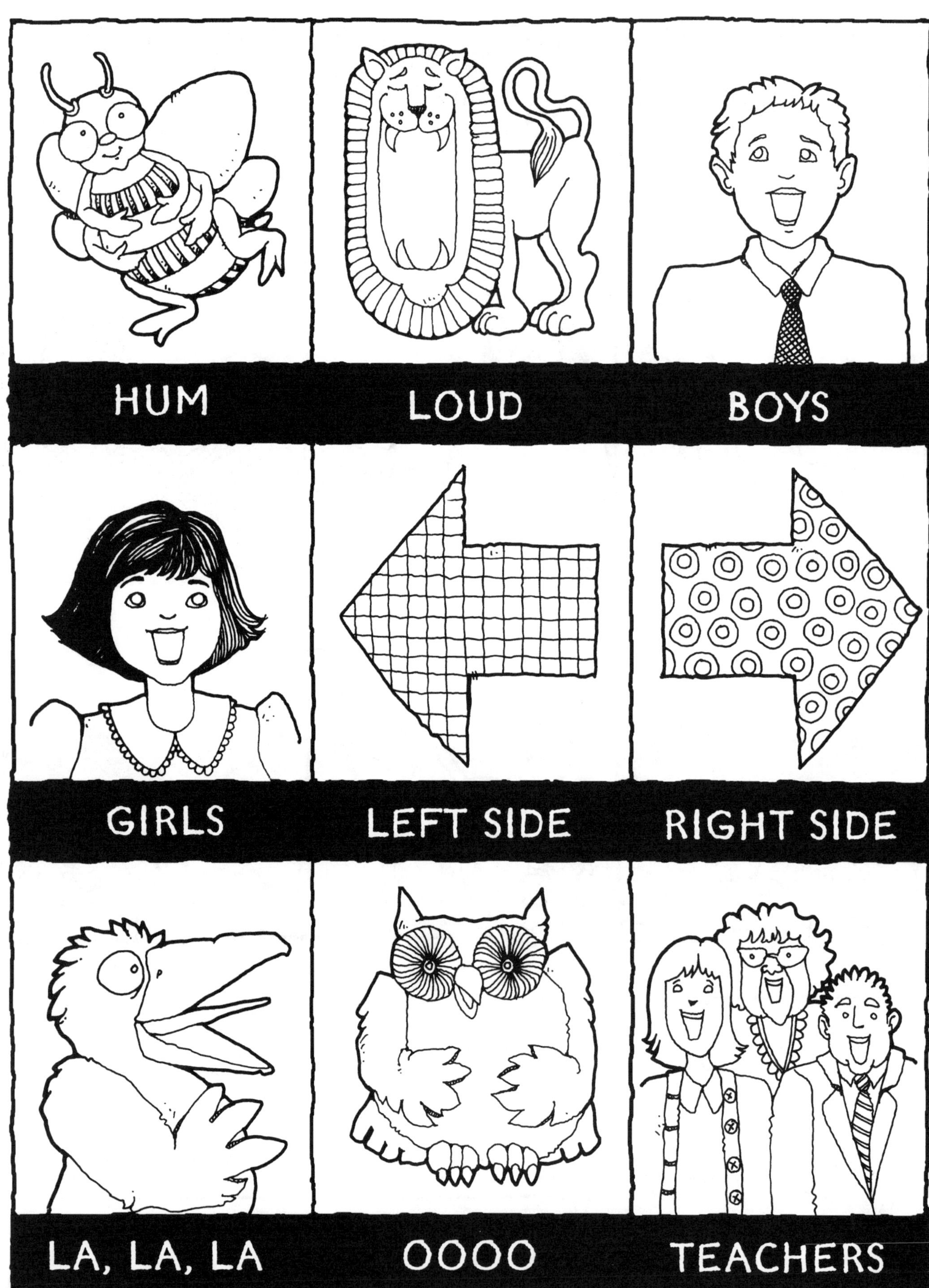
HUM
LOUD
BOYS
GIRLS
LEFT SIDE
RIGHT SIDE
LA, LA, LA
OOOO
TEACHERS

6 Heavenly Father Teaches Me How to Strengthen My Family

Children can instigate a number of activities that will strengthen families. They can encourage family scripture study and family prayer. They can help plan and participate in family home evening lessons and activities. They can help younger siblings get ready for church and be excited about going to Primary.

President Ezra Taft Benson said: "Dear children, our Heavenly Father sent you to earth at this time because you are some of His most valiant children. He knew there would be much wickedness in the world today, and He knew you would be faithful and obedient" ("To the Children of the Church," *Ensign*, May 1989, **p.**).

Of course, children alone should not have the responsibility of keeping a family together. That is the responsibility of the entire family. A family that enjoys activities together will naturally develop love and harmony. When that love is felt, children will be more willing to listen to their parents and choose the right. Parents will also be more willing to listen to the Holy Ghost and follow his promptings.

Use the activities on pages 28 through 31 to help the children learn how they can help strengthen their families.

Pages 28–29. Prepare a copy of page 28 for each child. Use an X-ACTO® knife to make slits along the dotted lines. Prepare enough copies of page 29 for each child to have as many figures as there are people in her family. Pass out the charts, figures, and a blank sheet of paper for each child. Have the children put glue around the edges of the chart and glue it to the blank paper. They may color in the words if time allows. Help the children write the name of a family member on each figure, then cut out the figures. Show the children how they can slide a figure through a slit in the chart, with the heads and arms hanging out, to assign responsibilities for family home evening.

Page 30. Prepare a copy of page 30 for each child. Send this chart home to be hung in a prominent place. Encourage the children to help their families do the things on the chart. (This is a personal family chart. Don't require it to be brought back for follow-up.)

Page 31. Prepare a copy of page 31 for each child. Instruct the children to use their scriptures to look up Mosiah 18:21, then find each of the words in that verse in this puzzle. Look up, down, across, and diagonally. Encourage the children to take the game home and share it with their families.

OBJECT LESSON

Topic: If we help each other stand, we won't fall

Objects: Cane, wheelchair, hearing aid, glasses, walker, or pictures of these items

Scripture: Ether 12:37

Show the children the cane, wheelchair, glasses, and so on. Explain how these items are used and how they help the person who needs them to do something better. Explain that all of these devices help us to overcome a specific physical weakness. Ask the children to think of weaknesses we might have that are not physical. Children might think of things like not being able to read very well, not being able to figure out math problems, being mean to others, not sharing, using language that is rude or unkind, and so on.

Explain that just as the items discussed above help us to overcome physical weaknesses, Heavenly Father has blessed us with many different ways to overcome other weaknesses. The most important thing he has given us is a Savior to atone for our sins. But he has also given us commandments to guide and direct us. He taught us to pray so we could communicate with him. He gives us peace through the Holy Ghost. He gave us families to protect and love us. He gave us teachers, leaders, church programs, and family home evening to help us strengthen our families.

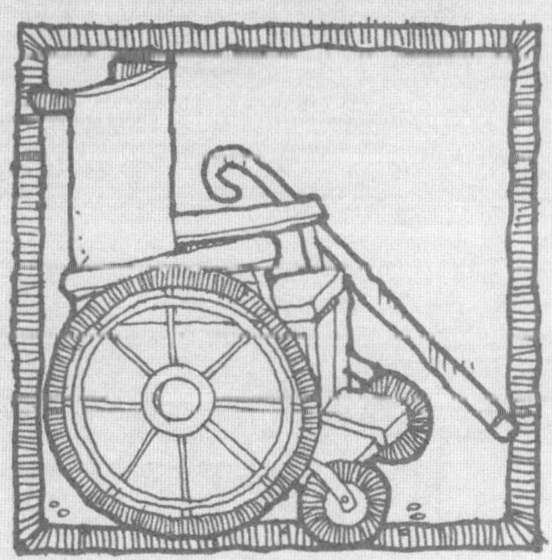

FAMILY HOME EVENING

CONDUCT	MUSIC
OPENING PRAYER	CLOSING PRAYER
LESSON	ACTIVITY
TREATS	AUDIENCE

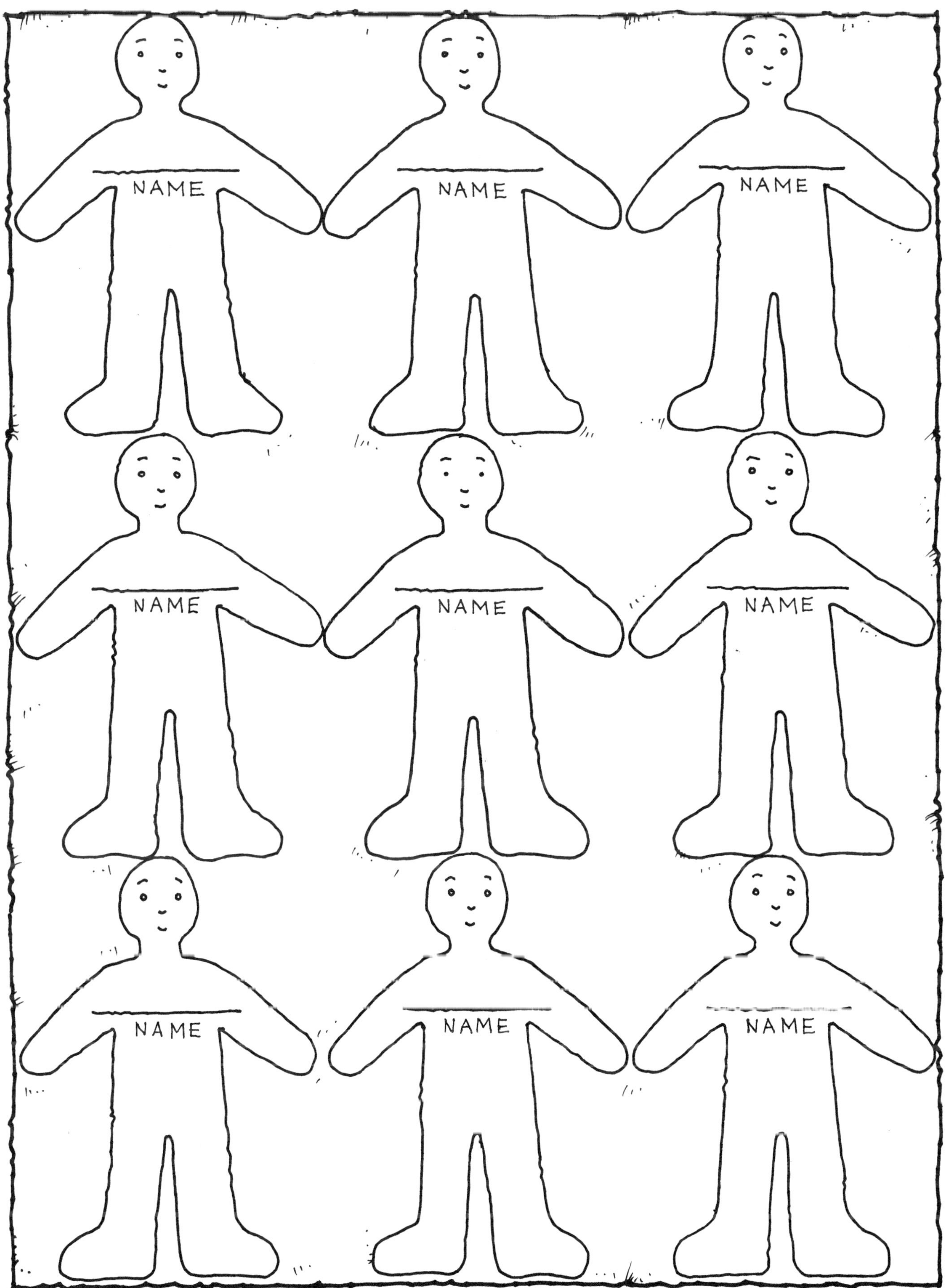
NAME
NAME
NAME
NAME
NAME
NAME
NAME
NAME
NAME

	FAMILY PRAYER	SCRIPTURE READING	CLEAN UP	HAPPY HELPER	SPEAK KINDLY	WHAT WOULD JESUS DO?
M						
T						
W						
TH						
F						
S						
SUN						

STRONG FAMILIES

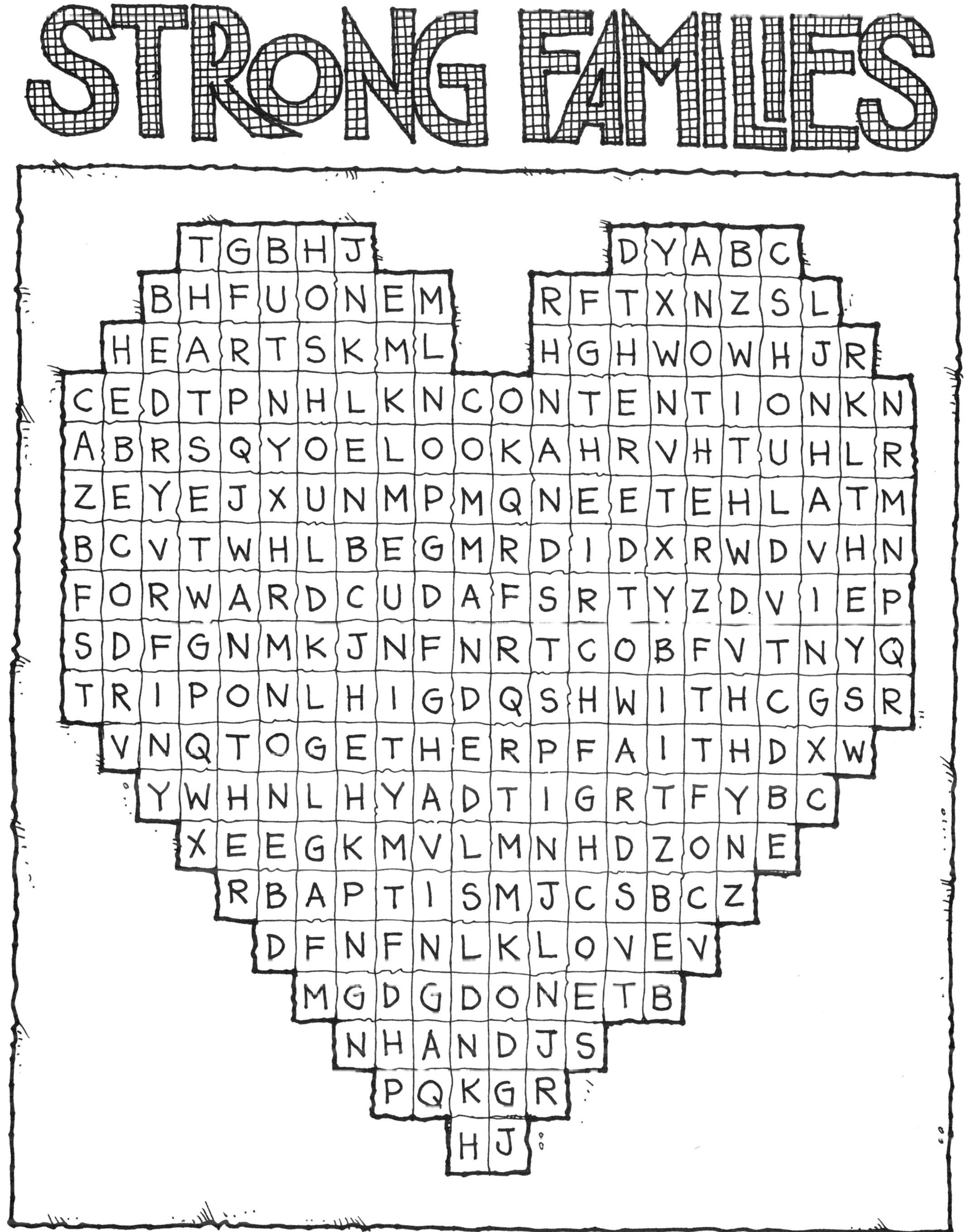

USE YOUR SCRIPTURES TO LOOK UP MOSIAH 18:21, THEN FIND EACH OF THE WORDS IN THAT VERSE IN THIS PUZZLE. LOOK UP, DOWN, ACROSS, AND DIAGONALLY.

7 Temples Unite Families

The temple is the house of the Lord. It is a holy sanctuary where sacred ordinances are performed for worthy members of the Church. These ordinances are also performed on behalf of our deceased ancestors. Only the home can compare with the sacredness of the temple.

Temple covenants and ordinances make it possible for us to be united for eternity and return to the presence of our Heavenly Father.

Use the activities on pages 33 through 36 to help the children understand how temples and temple work bind families together forever.

Page 33. Enlarge page 33. To fill in the boxes on the tree, research your own family history or that of a latter-day prophet. Show the children the tree and talk about family structure. If possible, show pictures of or share stories about the family members on your family tree. Other teachers, leaders, or ward members could dress in costume as one of your ancestors and pretend to be that person as you place each name on the family tree.

After the presentation, give each child his own copy of page 33 to fill in. Challenge the children to complete the family tree during family home evening.

Pages 34–35. Enlarge and make two copies each of pages 34 and 35. Color and cut out on the straight lines. Cover the pictures with squares of paper thick enough that you can't see through them. Number the squares, then hang the sets of squares on the board for a game of concentration. When a pair is matched, talk about how the picture pertains to the family history of the children in your Primary.

Page 36. Many family history records are written in other languages. They must be carefully translated and entered into computers or onto special forms. Use this game to illustrate this idea. Prepare a copy of page 36 for each child. Have the pianist play soft music (songs on pages 95, 188, and 199 of the *Children's Songbook* would be appropriate) in the background while the children decode the scripture and color the picture. Remind them to take it home to share with their families.

OBJECT LESSON

Topic: Temple work can protect our family

Object: Shoes of all kinds—work, dress, running, worn out, slippers, and so on

Scripture: Alma 13:16

Shoes are like families. They are made to protect us. Each kind serves a different purpose. Gather as many kinds of shoes as possible. Display them in pairs. Use the ideas suggested or make up your own according to your shoes and the needs of your students.

Dress shoes: We should be on our best behavior with our families.

Slippers: We should pray constantly in our families.

Work boots: Families can help us get tough jobs done with protection from dirt, stickers, and other harms.

Worn-out shoes: Our family members are reliable, dependable, and always there for us.

Snow boots: Families can protect us from harsh elements.

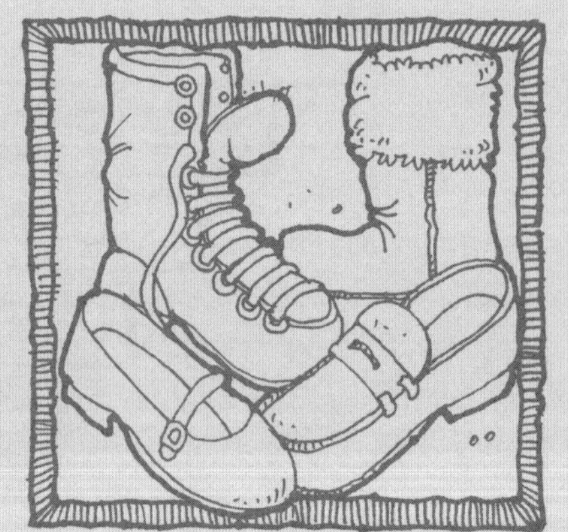

MY FAMILY TREE

FAMILY
MISSIONARIES
TEMPLE
COMPUTER
ANCESTOR
FAMILY
BAPTISM
WAGON
CAR
Beloved Father
BORN
DIED
MOTHER
BORN
DIED
ERIKSON
JOAN JEFF
BORN BORN
8·20·62 9·7·60
GRAVES

HISTORY

SCRIPTURES
PRAYER
PEDIGREE CHART
PEDIGREE CHART
BOAT
PLANE
TRAIN
JOURNAL
JOURNAL
N
S
MAP
MARRIAGE

TEMPLE WORK UNITES FAMILIES FOREVER

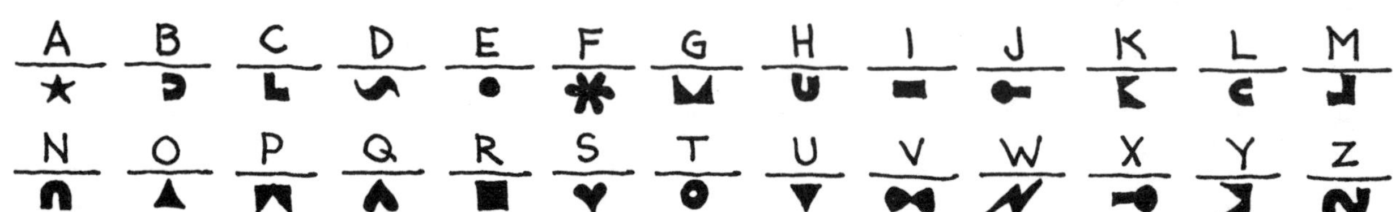

USE THE CODE ABOVE TO FILL IN THE BLANKS BELOW.
WHEN YOU ARE FINISHED YOU SHOULD BE ABLE TO READ THE WORDS IN HELAMAN 10:7

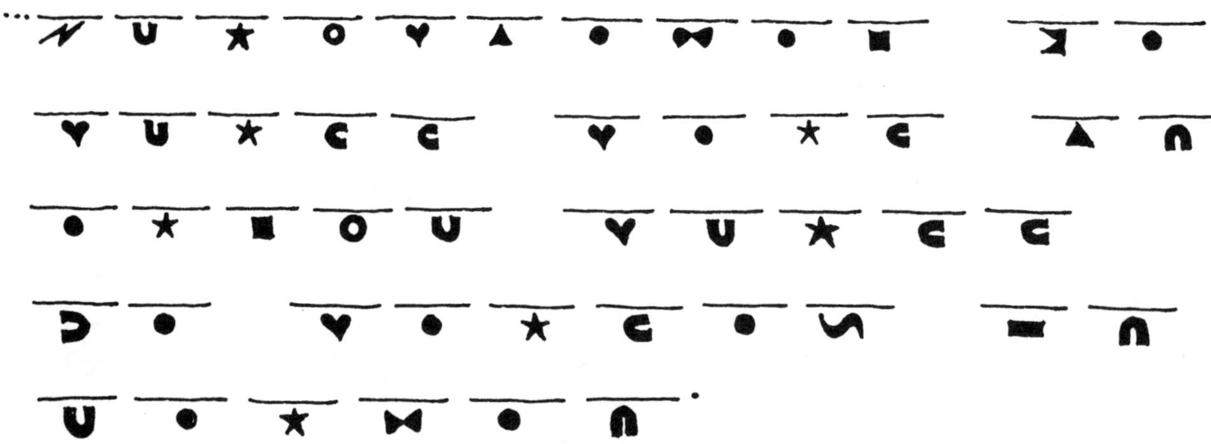

HELAMAN 10:7

8 Faith, Prayer, Repentance, and Forgiveness Can Strengthen My Family

Faith, prayer, repentance, and forgiveness are essential to a strong family and enable the members of that family to make wise choices and stay on the path toward our Father in Heaven.

Use the activities on pages 38 through 41 to teach children about the principles of faith, prayer, repentance, and forgiveness.

Page 38. Enlarge and color the maze on page 38. Talk about the difference between making simple mistakes or misunderstandings and making wrong choices. Discuss how the older and smarter we get, the more accountable we are for our choices. Talk about how making a good choice helps us want to make more good choices and how making bad choices makes us feel unhappy. Then discuss the steps of repentance listed on page 39. After your discussion, have the children help you with the maze by looking at the pictures and deciding if the children depicted in the pictures are making wrong or right choices. Talk about how the children depicted in the maze can repent of bad choices and get back on the right path, the path to happiness and Jesus. Make a copy for each child and remind her to share it with her family.

Page 39. Enlarge page 39. Cut out the footsteps and hide them around the room. Have children find them, one at a time, and bring them to the front of the room. Have another child put the footsteps in order. Talk about why repentance should follow that order. Ask the children what would happen if we skipped a step. Tell a personal story of repentance and forgiveness and bear your testimony of how you felt clean and happy after completing each step. Make a copy for each child to take home and share with her family.

Page 40. Prepare a copy of page 40 for each child. Have the pianist play soft music (songs on pages 96, 98, 99, 124, and 182 of the *Children's Songbook* would be appropriate) while the children work on the word search. Talk about Heavenly Father's plan—that we chose to come to earth, receive a body, and learn to make choices. Remind the children that if we have faith in Jesus, pray often, and repent, we will be forgiven. We will be happy, our families and Jesus will be happy, and people around us will be able to see and feel the spirit of Jesus Christ shining through us.

Page 41. Make a copy of page 41 for each child to complete in class or sharing time or to take home to share with her family. Remind the children to tell their families of Jesus' love, repentance, forgiveness, faith, and prayer.

OBJECT LESSON

Topic: Keep the good in and the bad out

Objects: Clean and dirty filters from a furnace, dryer, air filter, or oil filter

Scripture: 3 Nephi 24:18

Begin a discussion similar to the following: Have you ever cleaned out the lint trap of the dryer? It can get so clogged and so dirty that it isn't able to do its job. If we neglect the oil and air filters on our cars, serious, permanent, and costly damage can occur. Our family ties are the same way. If we hold grudges, speak unkindly, or neglect scripture study and family prayer, Heavenly Father's blessings, as well as his strengths and the power of the Holy Ghost, will have a difficult time helping us.

Display the dirty filters. The dryer filter will be the easiest to show how to clean. Remove the lint, explaining that all it is is small particles of dust collected together a bit at a time until nothing can penetrate the screen. When the lint is gone, look through the screen at the children, demonstrating how it is open for air to go through. Tell the children that bad media, bickering, fighting, faultfinding, blame, and so on are things that can clog our family filters. We can follow Jesus' teachings, obey his commandments, and listen to the promptings of the Holy Ghost and always have a way for the Spirit to reach us.

REPENTANCE WILL RETURN ME TO THE RIGHT PATH

LOOK AT EACH PICTURE ON THIS PAGE AND DETERMINE WHETHER OR NOT THE CHILD IS MAKING A GOOD CHOICE. IF THE CHOICE IS WRONG, CROSS THE PICTURE OUT AND WRITE DOWN WHAT THE CHILD CAN DO TO CORRECT HIS CHOICE. AFTER DOING THIS, FOLLOW THE PATH FROM THE CHILD AT THE TOP LEFT TO THE PICTURE OF JESUS.

5 Steps to Repentance

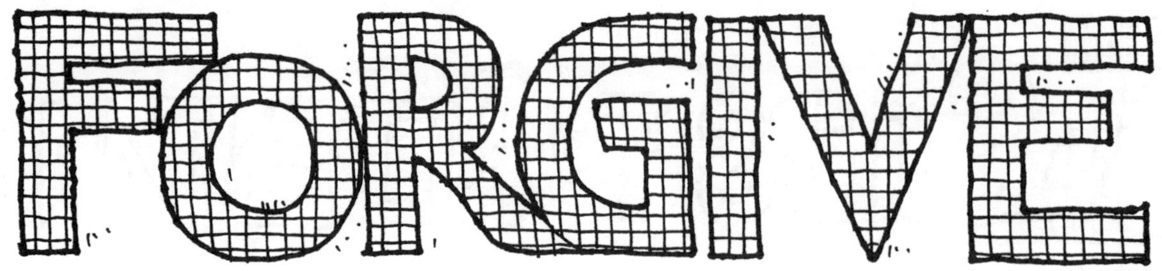

F	O	R	G	I	V	E	F	O	R	G	I	V	E	Y
O	I	F	F	B	Y	E	T	H	E	I	R	B	F	O
R	Y	E	O	C	F	O	R	G	I	V	E	D	C	U
G	H	D	R	N	O	T	E	H	F	A	T	H	E	R
I	G	F	G	T	R	E	S	P	A	S	S	E	S	F
V	J	N	I	N	G	Z	P	K	T	Y	G	A	M	O
E	L	E	V	P	I	J	A	W	H	O	L	V	N	R
K	M	I	E	Q	V	C	S	I	E	U	M	E	N	G
B	U	T	R	Y	E	A	S	L	R	R	P	N	F	I
T	S	H	W	V	T	L	E	L	W	I	L	L	O	V
T	R	E	S	P	A	S	S	E	S	R	Q	Y	R	E
H	V	R	X	X	F	O	R	G	I	V	E	O	G	B
E	F	O	R	G	I	V	E	M	S	Y	Z	U	I	Y
I	W	F	O	R	G	I	V	E	D	I	G	R	V	O
R	F	O	R	G	I	V	E	N	F	F	O	R	E	U

USE YOUR SCRIPTURES TO LOOK UP 3 NEPHI 13:14–15. FIND EACH OF THE WORDS IN THOSE VERSES IN THIS PUZZLE. LOOK UP, DOWN, ACROSS, AND DIAGONALLY. FIND THE WORD FORGIVE 12 TIMES.

CONNECT THE DOTS TO SEE TWO CHILDREN WHO ARE FOLLOWING JESUS' EXAMPLE.

9 Respect, Work, Love, and Wholesome Recreation Can Strengthen My Family

In "The Family: A Proclamation to the World," the First Presidency teaches us that "successful . . . families are established and maintained on principles of . . . respect, love, compassion, work, and wholesome recreational activities" (*Ensign*, November 1995, 102). Each of these principles will strengthen the family and help lead children and parents back to Jesus Christ.

Use the activities on pages 43 through 46 to teach children about the importance of respect, work, love, and wholesome activities.

Page 43. Prepare a copy of page 43 for each child. Talk about the four starting points on the handout: respect each other, love each other, work together, and play together. Discuss ways that families do these things. Have each child quickly tell about a favorite family fun time. Mention each scripture on the handout in response to their comments. Have the pianist play quiet music (songs on pages 138, 177, 188, 192, and 193 of the *Children's Songbook* would be appropriate) while the children complete the puzzle by crossing out every other letter in each strand and writing the remaining letters in the blanks below. Start with the first letter after the star.

Younger children who are unable to write can silently act out a chore, fun family activity, or an act of love or respect and have the other children guess what it is.

Pages 44–45. Prepare copies of pages 44 and 45 for each child. Tape the pages together or make them into a booklet (add empty pages for the children to draw on). Encourage the children to go for a family ride, hike, or walk. As they do so, the children can color or cross out the pictures of objects they find on the excursion.

You can also use these pages to play bingo or blackout in class while going on a pretend family ride. Make copies for each child, plus a copy you can color and cut out. Place the pictures around the room for the children to "spot" on their pretend trip.

Page 46. Prepare a copy of page 46 for each child. Talk about what things a family can do together for work and for entertainment. Ask the children to name a few things they would like to do with their families that they don't already do. Have the children take page 46 home to hang in a prominent place. Have them write down activities, service, and chores that they and their families can do together. Help them plan a special family home evening to talk about setting some of these goals.

OBJECT LESSON

Topic: Life keeps on going and going
Object: A wind-up toy that turns when it runs into an obstacle
Scripture: D&C 66:12

Obtain a battery-operated or wind-up toy that turns or reverses when it runs into an obstacle. Demonstrate the toy several times so that all can see and understand that the toy will turn or reverse in another direction so that it can keep going or progressing.

Talk about some of the obstacles in our lives that prevent us from making personal progress and are unexpected: illness, loss of job, bad choices, moving, new brother or sister, death of family member or friends, death of pet, and so on. Discuss how things hurt us physically or hurt our hearts. What can we do to find peace and happiness again? By knowing Heavenly Father's loving plan, we can go around obstacles, back up, and try again, moving ahead to find happiness.

COMPLETE THE PUZZLE BY CROSSING OUT EVERY OTHER LETTER IN EACH STRAND AND WRITING THE REMAINING LETTERS IN THE BLANKS BELOW. START WITH THE FIRST LETTER AFTER THE STAR.

RESPECT EACH OTHER★

LOVE EACH OTHER★

WORK TOGETHER★

PLAY TOGETHER★

RESPECT★ ___ _______ ___ _____ _______ ______
__ ____, ___ __ _____ __ ____ MATTHEW 7:12

LOVE★ ____ ___ ________; ____ _____ ______
___ JOHN 13:34

WORK★ ___ ____ _____ _____ ___ ___ ____
_____ __ ________ ALMA 36:25

PLAY★ _ _____ _____ _____ _____ ____
_ _________ PROVERBS 17:22

WHILE WE WERE OUT-
BUS

WE SAW...

THINGS WE DO TOGETHER

10 Prophets Teach Me How to Strengthen My Family

A prophet's work is to act as God's messenger and make His will known.

Through all time, prophets have given us messages concerning the family and how it can be strengthened. Ancient scripture tells story after story about families: Abraham and Isaac, Jacob and his sons, Lehi and his family, Alma and his sons, and so on. Latter-day revelation continues to confirm what we learn in the scriptures about the sanctity of the family. It also teaches us that the family can be sealed together for time and all eternity in a permanent relationship.

Use the activities on pages 48 through 51 to teach the children about the importance of following the prophets' counsel for families.

Pages 48–51. These pages can be used in a variety of ways:

• Enlarge and copy pages 48 and 50. Color and cut each square apart. Put the pictures in a paper sack and have one child at a time draw one out and decide whether it is an ancient prophet or a latter-day prophet.

• Prepare a copy of pages 50 and 51. Color and cut apart. Put the squares with prophet pictures in a sack and the squares with words on the board. Have one child at a time draw a picture from the sack and match it with the words on the board.

• Enlarge and prepare copies of pages 48 and 49, and 50 and 51 for each child. Cut apart. Glue the corresponding words to the back of each prophet picture. Punch a hole in the corner of each picture and put either a clasp ring or piece of yarn through the hole. Have the children use the booklet for answers to a "Prophets Guessing Game." The leader will ask questions such as, "I am thinking of an ancient prophet who built a tower so he could teach his people about families." The children will turn to the picture of King Benjamin.

• Make two copies of pages 48 and 50. Color and cut apart. Place on the board in a random order and cover each with a numbered square of paper. Play concentration. When a match is made, read the counsel from that prophet.

All of these games and activities can be played at home during family home evening, scripture study time, fun time, or put in the children's Sunday boxes (see next chapter).

OBJECT LESSON

Topic: Prophets make us strong
Object: Strips of paper (approximately 1x5 inches in size) with various prophet names on them
Scripture: 3 Nephi 12:11-12

Cut 12 to 15 strips of white paper, approximately 1x5 inches in size. Write the names of various Old Testament, New Testament, Book of Mormon, and latter-day prophets on them. Pass them out to the students. One at a time, have a student bring her strip of paper to the front of the room and place it on a table. Make a stack out of the strips, briefly discussing a teaching from each prophet as the strips are brought to the table. Once the stack is complete, have a child try to rip apart the stack. The stack will be strong and unbreakable. Explain to the children that the teachings of the prophets build upon each other to make an unbreakable foundation of gospel truths. If our families follow these teachings, we too will become strong.

MOSES
ISAIAH
JESUS
JOHN THE BELOVED
PAUL THE APOSTLE
NEPHI, SON OF LEHI
JACOB
ENOS
KING BENJAMIN
ALMA THE YOUNGER
CAPTAIN MORONI
HELAMAN
JESUS
MORMON
MORONI

PAUL THE APOSTLE

"Children, obey your parents in the Lord: for this is right."

(Ephesians 6:1)

JOHN THE BELOVED

"He that loveth his brother abideth in the light."

(1 John 2:10)

JESUS

"Love one another; as I have loved you."

(John 13:34)

ISAIAH

"And all thy children shall be taught of the Lord."

(Isaiah 54:13)

MOSES

"Set your hearts unto all the words which I testify among you . . . which ye shall command your children to observe to do, all the words of this law."

(Deuteronomy 32:46)

ALMA THE YOUNGER

"O, remember, my son, and learn wisdom in thy youth; yea, learn in thy youth to keep the commandments of God."

(Alma 37:35)

KING BENJAMIN

"And ye will not suffer your children that they go hungry, or naked; neither will ye suffer that they transgress the laws of God. . . . But ye will teach them to walk in the ways of truth and soberness; ye will teach them to love one another, and to serve one another."

(Mosiah 4:14–15)

ENOS

"I, Enos, knowing my father that he was a just man—for he taught me in his language, and also in the nurture and admonition of the Lord."

(Enos 1:1)

JACOB

"Their husbands love their wives, and their wives love their husbands; and their husbands and their wives love their children."

(Jacob 3:7)

NEPHI, SON OF LEHI

"I, Nephi, having been born of goodly parents, therefore I was taught somewhat in all the learning of my father."

(1 Nephi 1:1)

MORONI

"Come unto Christ, and lay hold upon every good gift, and touch not the evil gift, nor the unclean thing."

(Moroni 10:30)

MORMON

"My son, be faithful in Christ; and may not the things which I have written grieve thee, to weigh thee down unto death; but may Christ lift thee up, and may his sufferings and death . . . and his mercy . . . and the hope of his glory and of eternal life, rest in your mind forever."

(Moroni 9:25)

JESUS

"Pray in your families unto the Father, always in my name, that your wives and your children may be blessed."

(3 Nephi 18:21)

HELAMAN

"They had been taught by their mothers, that if they did not doubt, God would deliver them."

(Alma 56:47)

CAPTAIN MORONI

"Whosoever will maintain this title upon the land, let them come forth in the strength of the Lord, and enter into a covenant that they will maintain their rights, and their religion, that the Lord God may bless them."

(Alma 46:20)

JOSEPH SMITH
BRIGHAM YOUNG
JOHN TAYLOR
WILFORD WOODRUFF
LORENZO SNOW
JOSEPH F. SMITH
HEBER J. GRANT
GEORGE ALBERT SMITH
DAVID O. MCKAY
JOSEPH FIELDING SMITH
HAROLD B. LEE
SPENCER W. KIMBALL
EZRA TAFT BENSON
HOWARD W. HUNTER
GORDON B. HINCKLEY

LORENZO SNOW

"Honor your fathers and your mothers. . . . Be obedient and loving to them."

(*The Teachings of Lorenzo R. Snow*, 137)

WILFORD WOODRUFF

"Be kind to your brothers and sisters and all with whom you associate; kind words and good manners will cost you nothing and will add greatly to the happiness of those around you."

(*The Discourses of Wilford Woodruff*, 267)

JOHN TAYLOR

"We should live together in love."

(*Gospel Kingdom*, 283)

BRIGHAM YOUNG

"Let us live so that the spirit of our religion will live within us, then we have peace, joy, happiness and contentment, which makes such pleasant fathers, pleasant mothers, pleasant children."

(*Discourses of Brigham Young*, 204)

JOSEPH SMITH

"Children, obey your parents in all things, for this is well pleasing unto the Lord."

(*Teachings of the Prophet Joseph Smith*, 88)

JOSEPH FIELDING SMITH

"Each family unit, where the parents have been married for time and for eternity, shall remain intact through all eternity."

(*Doctrines of Salvation*, 2:67)

DAVID O. MCKAY

"Obedience is heaven's first law, and it is the law of the home."

(Conference Report, June 1919, 78)

GEORGE ALBERT SMITH

"In our homes . . . it is our privilege, nay, it is our duty, to call our families together to be taught the truths of the holy scriptures."

(Conference Report, April 1914, 12)

HEBER J. GRANT

"One of the greatest things that can come into any home to cause the boys and girls in that home to grow up in a love of God, and in a love of the gospel of Jesus Christ, is to have family prayer."

(Conference Report, October 1923, 7–8).

JOSEPH F. SMITH

"To be a successful father or a successful mother is greater than to be a successful general or a successful statesman."

(*Gospel Doctrine*, 285)

GORDON B. HINCKLEY

"Love is the very essence of family life."

(*Ensign*, May 1989, 67)

HOWARD W. HUNTER

"One of the keys to strong family life is family home evening."

(*The Teachings of Howard W. Hunter*, 43)

EZRA TAFT BENSON

"Our homes should be places of refuge, love, and harmony. Under the direction of the father, each family should have prayers, gospel study, and family home evenings."

(*Ensign*, January 1991, 5)

SPENCER W. KIMBALL

"The Lord has promised that if boys and girls and their parents are faithful in paying their tithing, he will pour out great blessings upon them."

(*Ensign*, November 1979, 4)

HAROLD B. LEE

"Happiness comes from unselfish service. And happy homes are only those where there is a daily striving to make sacrifices for each other's happiness."

(*The Teachings of Harold B. Lee*, 296)

11 Keeping the Sabbath Day Holy Can Strengthen My Family

The Sabbath is a day for man to rest from his labors, contemplate the word of God, and assemble for public worship. These are essential for a person's spiritual development. The existence of a weekly holy day safeguards us from earthly temptations and gives us a constant reminder of the need to be fed spiritually, personally, and as a family.

Sunday should be the day to slow down, make time for each other, and rekindle and share each other's company.

In addition to the activities that follow, you might want to find a shoe box and cover it with wrapping paper, magazine cutouts of families, or plain paper. Label this your "Sunday Box." Collect appropriate games, puzzles, stories, toys, pictures in flip charts, and other Primary activities to put in the "Sunday Box." Use the items in the box just for quiet Sunday times. The activities on pages 53 through 56 could all be placed in the box.

Page 53. This activity works best in a small classroom or family setting. The CD-ROM at the back of this book includes the bingo card on page 53, as well as five additional bingo cards. Print out as many of the cards as you need for your small group. Give each player one bingo card and a set of bingo markers. (Note that if you have more than six players, you will have more than one winner at a time.) For bingo markers, cut out 25 half-inch paper squares for each player. You can also use candy, pennies, buttons, or other objects for bingo markers.

Randomly call out the items on the card. Talk about each item and discuss why it is an appropriate Sabbath day activity. The first child with five markers in a row up, down, or diagonally calls out bingo. Send the copy of the card home with the child. Have him color the pictures as he does each sabbath activity depicted on the card.

Page 54. Prepare a copy of page 54 for each child. Have the pianist play soft music (songs on pages 23, 72, 73, 156, and 158 in the *Children's Songbook* would be appropriate) as the children cut out the word strips at the bottom of the page and glue them on the fingers and thumb. Remind the children to take the handout home to share with their families.

Page 55. Prepare a copy of page 55 for each child. Have the pianist play soft music (songs on pages 23, 72, 73, 156, and 157 in the *Children's Songbook* would be appropriate) while the children connect the dots to find a way to show our love to Jesus. Remind them to take the picture home to share with their families. If time allows, bear your testimony and encourage the children to bear theirs.

Page 56. Prepare a copy of page 56 for each child. Have the pianist softly play hymns about the Sabbath. Encourage the children to hum along as they draw and color a picture of their family in the frame. Be sure their names and the date are written at the bottom. Remind them to share the picture with their families and keep it in a scrapbook or journal.

OBJECT LESSON

Topic: Finding appropriate activities for Sunday

Objects: Tin cans, bottles, wadded paper, dirty socks, leaves, yellow paper circles with Sunday activities written on them

Scripture: Mosiah 13:16–19

Write appropriate Sunday activities on the yellow paper circles and place them on a flat surface. Write inappropriate activities on masking tape and attach the tape to the other objects you have collected. Place the objects on top of the yellow circles. One at a time, have the students choose an object and read the activity written on it. Have them tell if it is what Heavenly Father and Jesus had in mind when they asked us to keep the Sabbath day holy. Throw the objects away. Discuss how we are eliminating the messes that keep us unfocused on Sundays. When the yellow circles are uncovered, talk about how they help us and our families be strong and happy by choosing to keep the Sabbath day holy and choosing appropriate activities.

SABBATH DAY BINGO

MY TESTIMONY

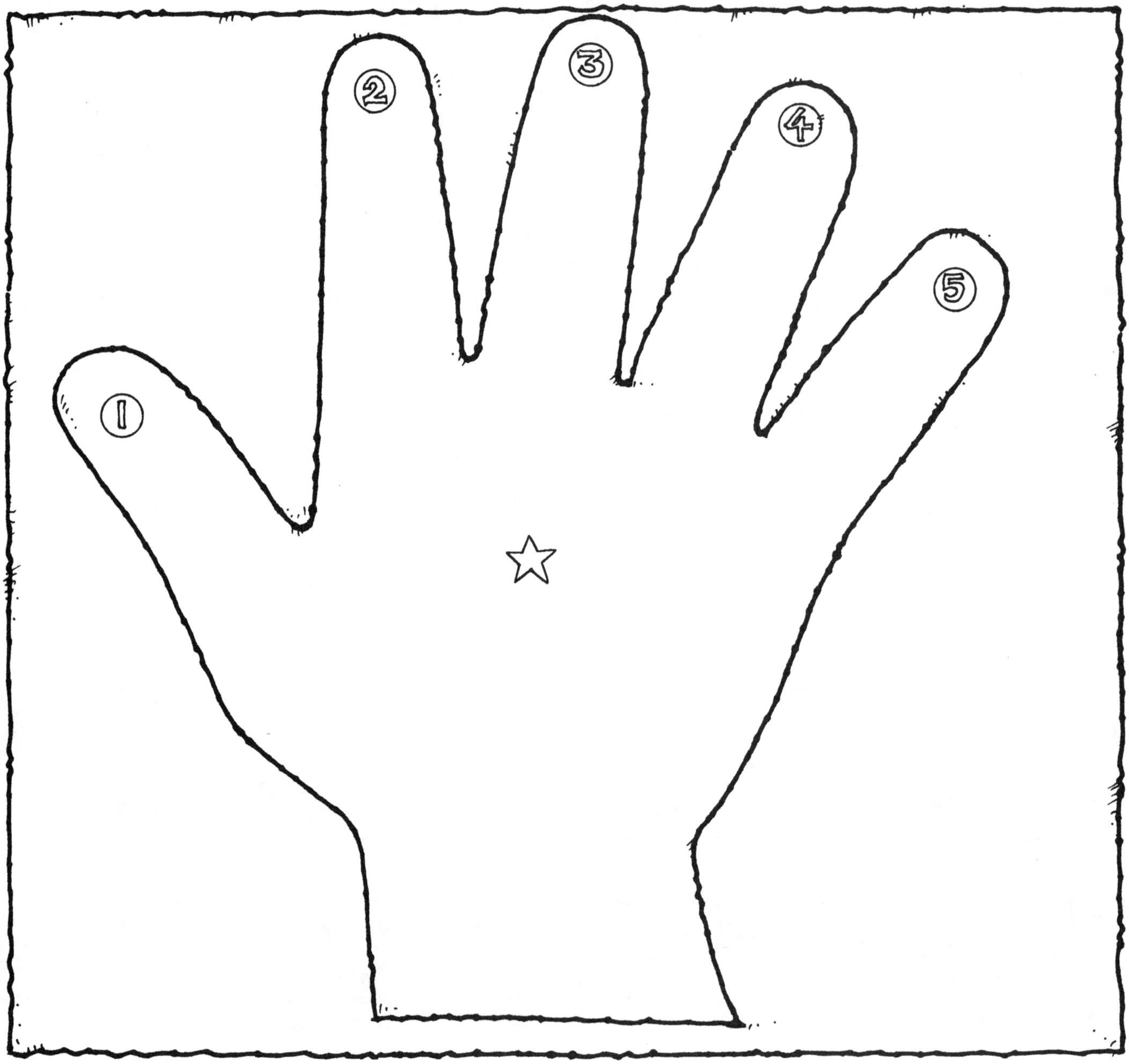

CUT OUT THE WORD STRIPS BELOW AND GLUE THEM ON THE FINGERS AND THUMB.

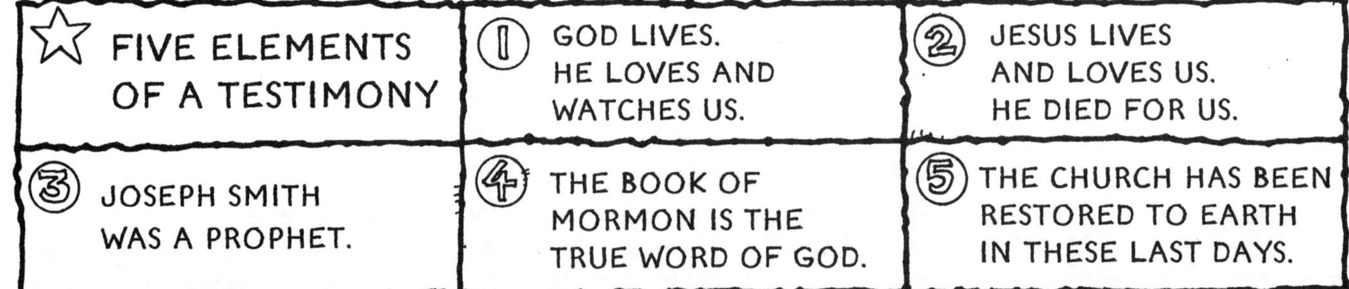

☆ FIVE ELEMENTS OF A TESTIMONY	(1) GOD LIVES. HE LOVES AND WATCHES US.	(2) JESUS LIVES AND LOVES US. HE DIED FOR US.
(3) JOSEPH SMITH WAS A PROPHET.	(4) THE BOOK OF MORMON IS THE TRUE WORD OF GOD.	(5) THE CHURCH HAS BEEN RESTORED TO EARTH IN THESE LAST DAYS.

CONNECT THE DOTS TO DISCOVER ONE WAY YOU CAN SHOW YOUR LOVE TO JESUS.

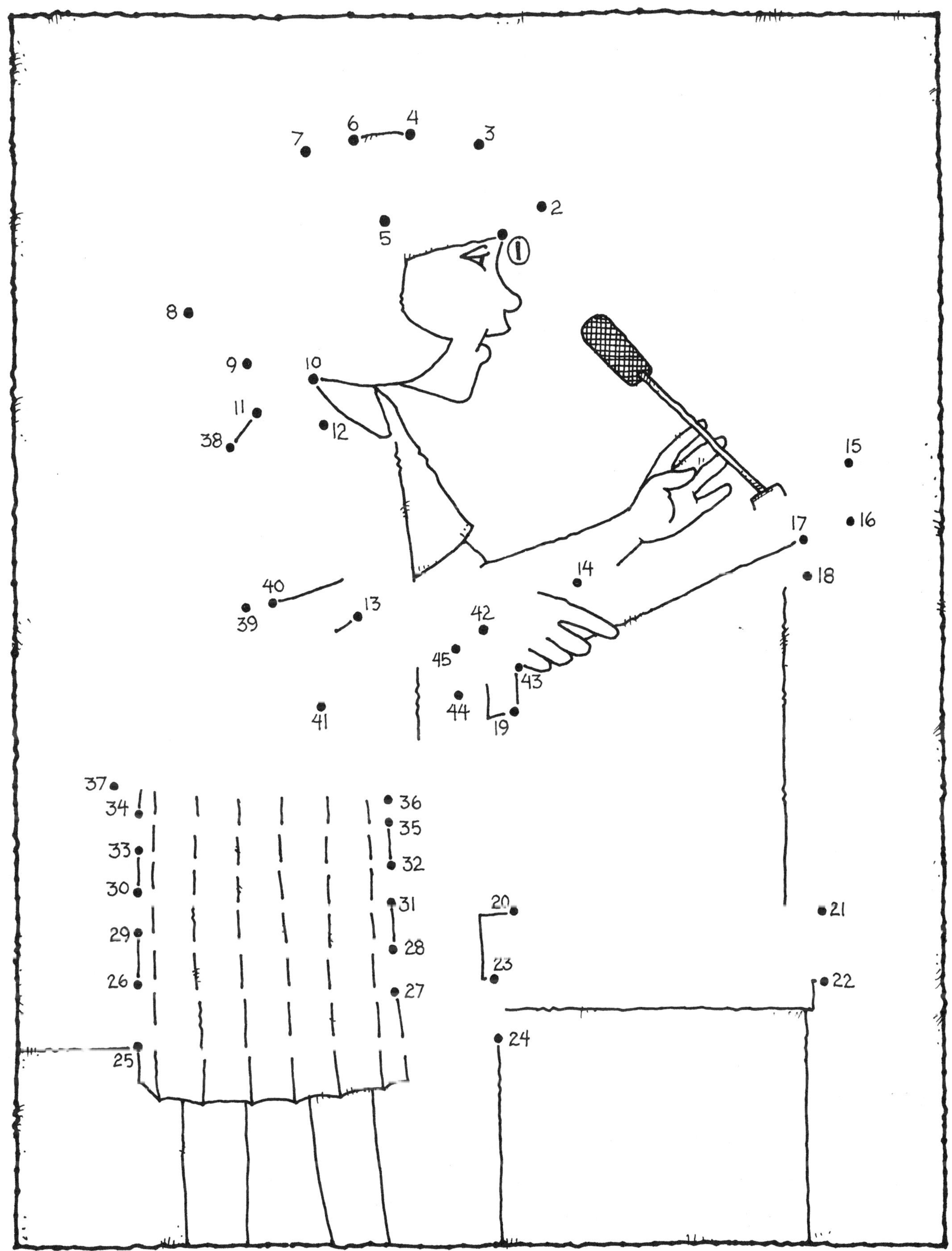

I AM THANKFUL FOR MY FAMILY

12 My Family Is Blessed When We Remember Jesus Christ

If we remember Jesus Christ every day, our families will be blessed and we will be better prepared to meet our Savior when he returns again to the earth. Remembering Jesus will also help us to choose to live as he did. If we choose to be kind and loving, others will love us and we will be happy.

Use the activities on pages 58 through 62 to teach the children the importance of remembering Jesus.

Page 58. Prepare a copy of page 58 for each child. Read Matthew 2:1–12 and discuss the gifts the wise men brought to Jesus. Explain that Mary and Joseph probably didn't have a lot of money to buy gifts for baby Jesus. The gifts the wise men gave him were probably the best material gifts he received in his life. We can't give Jesus material gifts like the wise men did. Ask the children what we can give him to show our love and appreciation for all that he gave us. Have the pianist play quiet music while the children use the handout to write down the things they would give Jesus if they could. Color and cut out the packages on the handout. Punch a hole where indicated and thread yarn through it. Bring a small tree that the children can hang the gifts on.

Page 59. Enlarge and color page 59. Cut a piece of paper the same size into puzzle pieces. Place the puzzle pieces over the picture of Jesus' family. One at a time, have a child come and remove a piece. Sing the child's favorite Christmas song or have her tell about a family Christmas tradition. Continue until the picture is uncovered. Give each child a copy of page 59 to color and take home and share with her family.

Page 60. Prepare a copy of page 60 for each child, then enlarge, copy, and color the page for use as a flip chart. To make the flip chart, cut out along solid lines, place the squares in order, punch holes at the top of each square, and fasten a metal ring or some string through the holes. As you display each picture in the flip chart, have a child read the scripture that goes along with the scene. Sing songs that go with the pictures. Give each child her own copy of the page to take home to share with her family. Suggest that she look at the pictures and read the scriptures Christmas morning with her family.

Page 61. Prepare a copy of page 61 for each child, then enlarge, copy, color, and cut out the pictures for use in a game. Punch a hole in the top of each picture. Hide the pictures around the room. Have the pianist softly play Christmas music as eight children find the pictures. Have them come to the front of the room, get in the correct order, and tell the story of the holy night Jesus was born in Bethlehem. Thread yarn or ribbon through the hole punched in the top of each picture and show the children how you can hang the figures from a Christmas tree, a lamp, a hanger (to make a mobile), or in the window.

Page 62. Prepare a copy of page 62 for each child. Talk about testimonies and encourage the children to take the page home, write their testimony on it, date it, and put it in a journal or scrapbook.

OBJECT LESSON

Topic: "I am the way"
Objects: An assortment of keys and locks
Scripture: John 14:6

Display the keys and locks you have collected. Talk about each kind and its use: car keys start a car, hotel keys unlock the door to your room, a combination lock keeps your bicycle safe or your gym locker closed, and so on. Explain that all of these keys will open a door or provide a "way" to get into something.

In John 14:6, Jesus said, "I am the way, the truth, and the life: no man cometh unto the Father, but by me." Discuss the ways that we can find "the way" through Jesus so that we may be blessed and strengthened on this earth and be with our families forever.

MY GIFT TO JESUS

JESUS HAS A FAMILY LIKE ME

LUKE 2:4–5
LUKE 2:7
LUKE 2:8–14
LUKE 2:15–17
MATTHEW 2:1–2
MATTHEW 2:11

MY TESTIMONY

GLUE
PHOTO
HERE

NAME

DATE